101
fantastic
things to do with your
Computer

TONY & LIZ WHEELER

TAG

THE 101 FANTASTIC TEAM

- Tony and Liz Wheeler

- For TAG: Jim Patterson and Will Wharfe

- Editorial and design: Paul Mason and Tim Mayer

- All artwork © Peter Greenwood

- Software development: Ultraviolet Design Limited

Copyright and Acknowledgements

Tag Learning Limited
25 Pelham Road, Gravesend, Kent DA11 0HU
First Published by TAG Learning Ltd. 2004

A CIP catalogue record of this book is available from the British Library

ISBN 1-902804-12-0

Printed in China by WKT Company Ltd

With thanks to seasoned 101ers, Ben Short, Tom Baird and Clare Oliver, who helped to make the original 101 titles.

The following company and product names, used in the book to assist with the installation of the accompanying CD-ROM, or safe running of your PC, or as software suitable for extension activities, may be trade marks or registered trade marks or trade names of their respective holders:

Apple, Macintosh, Mac, Mac OS, AppleWorks; Dance e-Jay; Dyno Park Tycoon; GarageBand; Greeting Card Factory; ImageBlender; KidPix Deluxe 3; Lego Creator; Microsoft, Windows, Office, Explorer; Mixman StudioXPro; MTV Music Generator; Netscape; Norton AntiVirus; Norton SystemWorks; Printshop Deluxe; Sim City; Simpsons Cartoon Maker; SMart; Sound Companion; Spy Kids 2; Storybook Weaver; The Codebreaker's Toolkit; The Zoombinis' Logical Journey; The Sims; Thinkin' Things 1, 2 and 3; Tony Hawk's Pro Skater 4.

CONTENTS

CREATIVE COMPUTING

Computers are fantastic! With the right software, your computer can be almost anything you want it to be: an incredible interactive painting set, a magical time machine, a spacecraft, even your own music or TV studio.

All your computer needs to get it going is your imagination and a little bit of know-how. Playing computer games is great fun, but there's so much more you can do.

Some people, especially grown-ups, think computers are difficult to use. Some people, particularly mums and dads, think that all children want to do with computers is play games. Some people, usually teachers, think computers should only be used for schoolwork.

This book and CD is for everyone who is interested in computers and wants to use them to do exciting, original and fun things. So let your imagination loose. There are (at least) 101 things to do.

Using a computer isn't difficult. To prove how easy it can be, we have included lots of useful ideas for projects to help you get started.

If your computer doesn't always behave itself, remember that it *is* only a machine. It's not as intelligent as a human being!

USING THE BOOK AND CD ROM

This book and CD-ROM were designed to be used together. The 101 CD will work with Windows computers and Apple Macintosh computers that use up to OS 9.2.2

People who use computers have made up a whole bunch of words for the hardware and software they use. You don't need to bother about most of them, but there are a few basics it is helpful to know about, especially when you go to buy software or new bits for your computer. You will find some useful information about computer hardware and software on the next few pages. And there is a glossary at the back of the book if you need to look up some of the most frequently used computer-speak for a short explanation.

Blah, blah, RAM...

Blah, blah, pixels...

Windows

If you have a Windows PC you will need:

- Pentium II 333MHz processor or better
- Windows 95 or later
- SVGA True Colour monitor; screen resolution 800x600 pixels
- 4MB graphics card or higher
- CD-ROM drive 4x speed minimum (8x recommended)
- sound card: SoundBlaster compatible
- speakers or headphones
- printer
- 32 MB memory RAM or higher (64 MB recommended)
- Internet connection to use the Internet links

Apple Macintosh

If you have an Apple Macintosh you will need:

- 200Mhz Power Mac, G3 processor or better
- Mac OS system 8.1 to 9.2.2
- 'Millions of Colours' monitor setting; screen resolution 800x600 pixels
- 4MB graphics card or higher
- CD-ROM drive 4x speed minimum (8x recommended)
- sound card: SoundBlaster compatible
- speakers (usually built-in) or headphones
- printer
- 32 MB available memory (RAM) or more (64 MB recommended
- Internet connection to use the Internet links

5

HARDWARE BIT

Even though this book is not about how computers work, it's worth spending a moment to make sense of the equipment you are using. It is useful to know what the various bits and pieces of your computer do, how they fit together, and how to use them most effectively.

THE BRAINY BIT

Your computer's 'brain' – the bit that does jobs like writing or drawing pictures for you – is a computer chip, packed inside a box called the CPU (Central Processing Unit).

Two important numbers give you your computer's digital IQ score, or how brainy it is. The first is the RAM (Random Access Memory). This tells you how big a computer's brain is. (You can usually add more RAM later on if you want to make your computer's brain bigger.) The second number to look out for is the microprocessor speed (or CPU speed). This tells you how quickly your computer can work things out.

COMPUTER CUPBOARDS

Your computer has to keep track of everything you put in it and keep it safely. This is called its 'memory'. Computers can store your files in lots of different ways.

The hard disk inside your computer is like a built-in filing cabinet, where you can keep your work safe until you need it again. Floppy disks, Zip disks and CD-R and DVD-R disks are like briefcases. They let you copy files from your computer and take them elsewhere.

Digital cameras and MP3 players mostly use memory cards to copy pictures and tunes on to your computer.

Normal CD-ROMs and DVDs store loads of information, which you can use on your computer. These disks are locked, so you can't record over them or add anything else to the disk.

SCREEN

The screen allows you to look inside your computer at all your files. There are two main types of screen. Older screens use a special ray gun called a Cathode Ray Tube (CRT) to shoot the picture onto the screen. This type of screen has a big box at the back to hold the ray gun. Newer screens are much flatter and thinner, and use special LCD (liquid crystal display) to make the picture.

The picture on your screen is made up from lots of little dots of different-coloured light. The smaller the dots, the clearer the picture. To use the 101 CD you need at least an 800x600 screen. To make it comfortable to work with your screen should be able to tilt and swivel.

MOUSE AND KEYBOARD

The mouse and keyboard let you tell your computer what to do by pointing and writing instructions. If you find it difficult to draw with a computer mouse you could try a graphic tablet, which uses a special pen.

INTERNET CONNECTION

With an Internet connection you can access the Net and find loads of useful information, do all sorts of exciting stuff, visit interesting places and keep in touch with your friends all over the world.

PRINTER

A colour inkjet printer is probably the best type to use. You can get all sorts of special papers for inkjet printers, which will allow you to make cards. There are even iron-on transfers you can print and use to make your own designer t-shirts.

e-ideas
Activity No.99

SOFTWARE STUFF

Your computer uses two main types of software. The first is its system software, which allows it to work. The second is the software tools that let you write, draw and do lots of other tasks on your computer.

SYSTEM SOFTWARE

The two most common types of system software used in homes and schools are Microsoft Windows and Apple Macintosh OS.

TOOLS

Software tools give you a blank screen with all sorts of different controls to add or make your own stories, pictures, videos, music or even sums. Integrated packages, like Microsoft Office or AppleWorks, are good because they combine lots of different tools that all work together.

Software tools your computer should let you work with:
- text (word processing)
- pictures (painting and drawing)
- numbers (spreadsheet)
- data (database)
- animation and video

READY REFERENCE

Some software is full of information with lots of pictures, text and video clips. These titles are like reference books with an added dimension – a great help for homework!

- encyclopaedia
- atlas
- picture/media libraries

COMPUTER GAMES

Even grown-ups have to admit that some computer games are really quite good! Choose titles that set you a different challenge each time you use them, and do not have a fixed or predictable outcome. We enjoy these games:

- The Sims
- Tony Hawk's Pro Skater 4

ACTIVITY SOFTWARE

Lots of software combines tools and information in educational activities that can be completed on screen. Some of our favourites are:

- The Zoombinis' Logical Journey
- Thinkin' Things 1, 2 and 3
- Dance e-Jay (PC) and GarageBand (Mac)

Always check with a grown-up before you download or install new software onto your computer.

UTILITIES

Some software adds extra features called 'utilities' to your system. There is special screen saver software, and tools to tidy up your files. To protect your files from damage, there's anti-virus software.

- disk utilities: Norton SystemWorks.
- anti virus: Norton AntiVirus.

GETTING STARTED

You should not need to install the 101 CD on your computer's hard disk. Instead, just pop it in the CD drive. The screens on the right should appear: just click on an activity you want to have a go at. If 101 does not run automatically, follow the instructions below:

Running 101 on Windows

101 should run automatically on Windows machines from Windows 95 onwards, once the disk has been put into the CD drive.

If 101 won't run:

1 Open 'My Computer' and double-click the CD-Rom icon.

2 Double-click on '101 Things.exe' to run the disk.

Running 101 on Mac OS

101 should run automatically on Mac OS machines up to OS9.2.2 once the disk has been put into the CD drive.

If 101 won't run:

1 Double-click on the 101 icon.

2 Double-click on the '101 Things' file to run the disk.

Click here to
return to
the main menu.

 Click here to
quit.

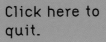 Click here to get
help: point your
cursor over a
button to get an
explanation.

Click on an activity to play

 Click here to bin
something or
start again.

 Click here
to print.

 Click here to
save your work
to your
computer.

 Click here to
open a saved
file.

 Click here to
export your
work as an
image.

 Click here to
go on to the
next thing.

 Click here to
go back.

 Click here to
undo your work.

USING THE 101 ACTIVITIES

Using the 101 activities is really
simple. Throughout the activities
there are buttons to press to move
around easily.

GENERAL CONTROLS

Every screen in the 101 disk uses some of
the controls shown on the left. They will
help you to navigate your way round the
disk, make changes to what you've
done, and save or print your work. You
can even throw away your work on some
activities and start again!

SPECIAL CONTROLS

Each activity also has its own buttons
for you to use. Use the 'help' button to
find out about these. Click on the
lifebelt, and explanations will appear
where you point the cursor.

USEFUL STUFF

As you get used to working with your computer you pick up all sorts of tricks and techniques. Here are some useful hints and tips we wish someone had told us when we first used a computer!

COPY AND PASTE

Make a small design in your painting program. Select your design and copy it. Paste and position it over and over again to create mosaic patterns. You could also copy and paste clips of video or sound to create interesting effects.

SCALE AND RESIZE

If your picture is the wrong size you can use your painting programme to squash or enlarge it, or make it a completely different shape. Record your voice onto your computer, then squash the sound files sideways. You'll sound like a monster or a mouse.

ROTATE AND REFLECT

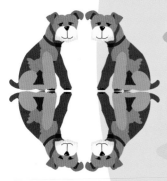

Try rotating or reflecting your design to create more interesting effects. If you reflect a sound or video file on your computer it will play backwards.

SAVE A SCREEN OR PICTURE

You can easily keep things you have created on your computer by saving your screen. Make sure the screen or picture you want to save is showing and then:

Windows:
● Press the print screen button and then paste the image into your paint package.

Macintosh:
● Press down the 'shift', 'Apple', and '3' keys. This creates a file called 'Picture 1' on your hard disk, which you can open with your paint package and copy into your design.

SCAN AN IMAGE

If the picture you want isn't already on your computer, see if your school or a friend has a scanner you can use. This makes a copy of your picture that you can store on disk. You can scan all sorts of things – photos, magazines, even wallpaper!

DIGITAL CAMERAS

If you can't find a scanner, someone is bound to have a digital camera you can borrow. This takes special pictures you can use on your computer and copy into your designs.

RECORDING YOUR OWN SOUNDS

Windows and Mac computers are similar. To record a sound:

- Many computers have built-in microphones. If yours does not, plug one in.
- Open the 'sounds' control panel.
- Check everything is working (a row of little lights should light up when you make a noise).
- Click the 'record' button, make your noise, then click 'stop'.
- Give your sound a name and save it to your hard disk.

Once you have collected your sounds you can use software like Sound Companion to edit and distort them:

You could use your computer to create:
- musical clips
- wacky sound effects
- voiceovers
- weird voices

- Copy and paste a clip of sound over and over again to create digital scratches.

- Flip a recording inside out and hear yourself talk backwards.

- Stretch and squeeze a sound to make it growl or squeak (great fun with voices!).

E-IDEAS MACHINE

Everyone has days when they're bored, with nothing interesting to do, right? Not any more: not with the e-ideas machine! It really does have 101 fantastic things to do (honest, we've counted) - just like it says on the cover!

Use e-ideas for:

- relief of extreme boredom
- entertainment of friends
- livening up wet Saturday afternoons
- a good excuse for not tidying your bedroom
- ideas for other things to do on your computer

ALL YOU NEED IS:

- a computer and the **101 Fantastic Things** CD
- some spare time

GET STARTED!

 1 Set your level of boredom and tell the ideas machine whether you want to use the idea indoors or outdoors.

 2 Select player numbers. You can play on your own or with your friends and family.

 3 Click on the lever. Your idea is ready to roll! If you want a different idea, just click again!

 4 Or you can click on the 'joke' button to be cheered up by a joke. Watch out for the elephants, though!

PLAY AWAY

There are 101 ideas for:

- Fantastic projects.
- Fun things to do with or without your computer.
- Hilarious jokes – click on the green button for the punch line!
- Either working from the screen or printing and playing later.

MIX IT UP

- Print out lots of ideas and spin a bottle/shuffle/pick one from a hat to choose which one to do.
- Liven up your diary with a different fun thing to do each day.
- Make up your own things to do and send them to your friends.
- Type your name/hobby/pet into an Internet search engine and see what happens...
- Set up an Internet treasure hunt: collect some clues from different websites and see if your friends can follow the trail you set them to the treasure or prize.

Taking it further

Do you have a talent for coming up with good ideas?

Look out for these titles:

- SMart
- KidPix Deluxe 3
- Lego Creator

E-CARDS

"Hi", "How's it going?", "Happy Birthday!". It's amazing just how many greetings we send. Why not use your computer to design and send all sorts of digital greetings to your family and friends?

Use e-cards to:

@ send a festive greeting (e.g. Christmas or Divali)
@ say 'Happy Birthday'!
@ cheer someone up
@ send a valentine
@ say a big 'Thank you'!

ALL YOU NEED IS:

● a computer and the **101 Fantastic Things** CD
● something to celebrate, and someone to share it with

GET STARTED!

1 Choose a theme for your card:
● Use the left and right arrows to find a category, like Christmas or Valentines.
● Click to choose a background.

2 Add some art:
● Drag and drop pictures to choose and position them on your card.
● Put unwanted pictures in the bin to get rid of them. Click on the bin to start from scratch.

3 Add a message: type your greeting in the box at the bottom. Use the controls to change colour and size.

4 Save your e-card and send it to someone special.

HAPPY WESAK

HAPPY DIWALI

HAPPY EID

PLAY AWAY

Once you are happy with your e-card you could:

● Print and send it through the post.

● Send it attached to an e-mail message.

OTHER THINGS TO DO

● Make cards for celebrations around the world. Then send someone a surprise greeting!

● Make up your own celebrations. What about pets' day, brother-and-sister day, no-homework day, pocket-money day...

Taking it further

Why not offer your services to your family and friends, to earn extra pocket money at Christmas or other special occasions?

Look out for these other titles to extend your creative talents:

● Printshop Deluxe

● Greeting Card Factory

● ImageBlender

E-MUSIC MACHINE

Ever wanted to be your own pop idol? Even if you can't play a musical instrument or sing very well, the answer might be at your fingertips. Why not use your computer to put together your own block-rocking beats?

Use the e-music machine to:

- make up your own tunes
- take samples from elsewhere
- mix different tracks together
- play it back (loud!) at home
- send music to your friends on CD or e-mail

ALL YOU NEED IS:

- musical inspiration
- someone to listen to your tune

GET STARTED!

1 Choose a melody for your tune.

2 Add other sounds and effects (drums, drum loops, vocals, DJ effects or miscellaneous) by dragging them into the relevant rows.

3 Click on the play icon at any time to play your tune.

4 Make adjustments by moving your notes around on the screen.

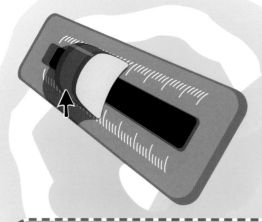

PLAY AWAY

Now your tune is ready to play. Stardom beckons!

- Press the arrow to play your tune.
- Press loop to loop your tune.
- Press the save button to save your tune.

Short of ideas?

- listen out for catchy music in adverts and TV trailers
- borrow tiny bits from other tunes (make sure they <u>are</u> only tiny bits!)
- grab some clip sounds off the Internet to use as instruments
- use your computer's microphone to record sounds to use as instruments

OTHER THINGS TO DO:

- Create a jingle for your own radio station.
- Create a theme tune for each of your friends/family/pets.
- Send your creations to a record company.
- Create your own recording label.

Taking it further

Think you might be heading for a career in the music industry and want to take it further?

Look out for these titles:

- Dance e-Jay
- MTV Music Generator
- Mixman StudioXPro
- Sound Companion

E-CARTOONS

"ZAP!", "POW!", "BIFF!". Cartoons are a great way to tell a story. Check out your favourites and look more carefully than usual, to see how they tell their story.

Use e-cartoons to:

- give your friends and family a laugh
- liven up boring homework tasks, or work out your ideas for essays and projects
- keep a cartoon diary
- explain how something works in pictures

ALL YOU NEED IS:

- a computer and the **101 Fantastic Things** CD
- a story to tell

GET STARTED!

1 Plan your story or joke to fit into 4 pictures.
- Make sure you have a beginning, middle and a punch line to end.

2 Click on the first frame: drag and drop to choose from the images on screen.
- Use the tools to change the images on screen or draw your own.

3 Add some speech bubbles or sound:
- Click on the style of speech bubble.
- Drag and drop into position.
- Type in text for each of your bubbles.

4 To make the next picture, click on the next box along the top of the screen.

PLAY AWAY

Print out your cartoon strips, or add them as attachments and send them by e-mail.

OTHER THINGS TO DO:

- Tell longer stories by combining several strips.
- Publish your stories in instalments and keep your friends on tenterhooks. Remember to end each instalment on a cliffhanger so that they will want to find out what happens next!
- Use animation software to bring your cartoon strip to life.
- Record your own sounds for each frame and import them.

Taking it further

All films start life as a comic strip known as a storyboard. Use e-cartoons to jot down your ideas for the next big blockbuster!

Look out for these titles:

- Storybook Weaver
- Simpsons Cartoon Maker

E-BRAINTEASER

Bored with board games and shoot-'em-ups? Then why not design your own digital challenge! E-brainteaser presents a great puzzle game to get you thinking.

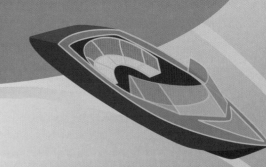

Use the e-games to:

@ test your problem-solving skills
@ put your friends to the
  e-brainteaser challenge
@ play solo against your computer

ALL YOU NEED IS:

- a computer and the **101 Fantastic Things** CD
- a logical mind for solving challenges
- to decide what style of game to play

GET STARTED!

1 Click on the e-games icon.

2 Decide on the style of game. Feeling racy? Click on the motorbike. For spacecraft click the spaceship button, or choose cars or planes.

3 Place four of your craft into the first line of the grid.

4 Are they parked opposite the correct dock? To find out, click on the flashing green light.

5 If they're all right first go, you're a genius! If not, try again.

PLAY AWAY

Use logic to solve the challenge in as few guesses as possible:

● Green tells you one of the right craft is in the right place.

Yellow tells you the right craft is in the wrong place.

● Red is the wrong craft altogether.

You can send your friends an e-mail brainteaser by clicking 'create game for a friend'. Pick an answer that might confuse them, then send it to their e-mail address. See if they can solve your challenge!

OTHER THINGS TO DO:

● Set up a challenge league. Find out who's quickest, and who can use least attempts.

● Check out free games on the Internet (e.g. Channel 4 Grid Club).

Taking it further

Look out for these other titles where you can create your own challenges:

● Tony Hawk's Pro Skater 4
● The Sims and Sim City
● Dyno Park Tycoon

E-SECRETS

Shush! Walls have ears, and your secrets may not be safe! Fortunately your computer can help, by letting you make coded messages that can only be unlocked with a special key.

Use e-secrets to:

- pass on secret tactics to your team
- share secret formulas, or recipes for snacks
- send secret answers to quizzes and crosswords

ALL YOU NEED IS:

- a computer and the **101 Fantastic Things** CD
- a top-secret message

GET STARTED!

1 Add a secret: make sure no one is looking over your shoulder!
- Type your secret message into the text box

2 Choose a code format: click to choose a letter or code number
- Use the arrows to spin the wheel, then set the code key and lock the wheel.

3 Click the code button to code your message.
- Your message will appear in code.

4 Send the code to a friend by e-mail – the key will appear in the subject line.

PLAY AWAY

To decode your message you will need the right code key (e.g. I for P)

- Paste a coded secret into the text box.
- Use the code wheel to set the correct code key for the secret message.
- Click 'decode'.

MIX IT UP

- Find out more about codes and secret messages (e.g. cipher, Morse or semaphore).
- Print out the code wheel screen, carefully cut out the 2 wheels and use them to create secret messages when you are away from your computer.
- Work out other ways to hide messages (writing backwards, using mirrors, invisible ink, using pictures).

Taking it further

It's not just spies and secret agents who use codes and secret messages!

Look out for these titles:

- *The Codebreakers Toolkit* (a CD-Rom and book by Simon Singh)
- Spy Kids 2

SITTING COMFORTABLY?

When you are playing with your computer, it's easy to lose all track of time. Sitting in one position and making the same movements over and over again can strain your body. Luckily, there are lots of common-sense things you can do to make sure you don't get a computer-related injury!

EYES AND EARS

● Do not sit too close to the screen.

● Make sure lighting is not reflecting off your screen.

● Look away from the screen regularly.

● If you are using headphones, don't turn them up too loud.

WRISTS AND HANDS

● Make sure you are sitting in front of your computer.

● Keep your elbows at the same height as the keyboard.

● Use a wrist support.

● Sit up straight so you are not resting any weight on your hands or wrists.

LOOKING AFTER YOUR BACK

● Use a chair with height adjustment and make sure you can reach everything without twisting or stretching.

● Sit up straight in your chair with your feet resting flat on the floor.

● Take regular breaks. Some computers allow you to set an alarm to warn you to get up and walk about, to stretch your legs and arms!

LOOKING AFTER YOUR COMPUTER

Spare a thought for your computer too: it's not just you that needs looking after! Even though they are pretty tough, there are some things you need to do to make sure your computer – and the files you create – work smoothly.

Slips and spills
It's very easy to knock drinks and snacks over. A little slip could seriously damage your keyboard, mouse or disks. Keep messy stuff well away from your computer.

Heat and dust
Computers work so hard they get very hot and need special fans to keep them chilled out. Keep them away from high temperatures. Dust can be a problem too and should be avoided.

Screen burn-out
If you leave the same picture on your screen for a long time it can cause damage. Screen savers automatically turn your screen off when it is not being used.

Computer viruses
It is possible for nasty programs called viruses to get into your computer without permission, especially if you use the Internet a lot. These programs can damage or even destroy your files. Use anti-virus software to check for viruses before you load or open any new files.

MANAGING YOUR WORK

You will soon have lots of your own files, which can easily get lost. Create a special folder on your hard disk to store your own work. Make sure you always save your files in it!

BACKING UP

Even though you have saved your work, it is worth making another copy and storing it somewhere else, just in case the original gets lost or damaged. Better safe than sorry!

PLAYING SAFE ONLINE

Once you are connected to the Internet, you can explore all sorts of exciting places and keep in touch with your friends all over the world. The **101 Fantastic Things** website has a collection of links to some of the most exciting sites in cyberspace.

YOU WILL NEED:

● Internet connection and Internet account

● Web browser (such as Microsoft Explorer, Netscape)

GET STARTED!

1 Never use the Internet with your computer without asking permission first from a **grown up.** Launch your browser and connect to the Internet.

2 Type in www.taglearning.com/101fantastic

3 Choose from the menu to zoom to the fantastic digital attractions.

Don't plug cables into your computer unless you're sure they're the right ones. Mistakes can be disastrous!

I am
a tall
dark handsome
prince
☺

PLAY SAFE!

The Internet is a public place. Follow these rules to make sure you stay safe.

- Never give anyone your personal details (name, home address, e-mail address, telephone number, school).
- Never make arrangements to meet anyone on the Internet.
- Be careful! People online may not be who they say they are.
- Remember everything you read online may not be true.
- Always make sure a grown-up knows what you are doing.

SHARING STUFF

It's easy to share your projects with others. The Fantastic Things CD saves your projects so that they will work on most other computers. The files are small enough to be attached to an e-mail message and sent over the Internet. The only software your friends will need are Quicktime and Shockwave, both available free on the Internet.

GLOSSARY

Application (or program)
Software that contains all the instructions your computer needs in order to do a particular kind of task.

Attachment
Any file that is sent with an e-mail message. It could be a picture, sound or movie.

Backup
A second copy of your work, kept in case the original gets lost or damaged.

Broadband
A fast Internet connection, which allows you to look at movies and big files online, and to download information quickly.

Browser
Software that allows your computer to explore the Internet. It's important to have the most up-to-date version available, so you can use all the latest gizmos on your favourite site.

CD-Rom
A compact disk used to store computer data. CD-Roms are locked, so you cannot copy your own files onto them.

CD-R
If you want to record onto a CD make sure it is a CD-R. The R means 'recordable'.

Download
When you copy e-mails or other files onto your computer through your Internet connection.

E-mail
A way of sending messages to other computers all over the world, using an Internet connection.

File format
Special code for the different ways your computer stores information about files. For example, you can use 'Jpeg' for pictures, 'Mpeg' for sound and 'Quicktime' for movies.

Hardware
All the bits of solid machinery that make up a computer: the CPU (see page 6), disk drives, screen, keyboard and mouse.

Internet
A network of millions of computers all over the world connected together through phone lines.

Modem
A special piece of equipment that connects your computer to a telephone line. Many computers have a modem inside them.

Off-line
If your computer is not connected to the Internet it is off-line.

Online
If your computer is connected to the Internet it is online, so you can connect to the World Wide Web and send e-mail messages.

Software
The instructions that tell a computer what to do.

World Wide Web
The network, or web, of information published on digital pages and accessed through the Internet.

Virus
A nasty program that gets into your computer without you knowing and which can destroy or damage your files.

USEFUL ADDRESSES

TAG Learning Ltd.
25 Pelham Road
Gravesend
Kent DA11 0HU
www.taglearning.com

BECTA (British Educational Communications and Technology Agency)
Millburn Hill Road
Science Park
Coventry CV4 7JJ

DfES Parent Centre
Public Enquiry Unit,
Sanctuary Buildings,
Great Smith Street,
London SW1P 3BT

Childnet International
Head Office, Studio 14
Brockley Cross Business Centre
96 Endwell Road
London SE4 2PD

INDEX

32